"Fundo's Animal Alphabet"
by Garry Atkinson and Ayana Davis

Copyright © 2013 by Garry Atkinson
Editing by LaKela Atkinson, www.fortheloveofwordsonline.com

www.FundoPress.com

For my niece and goddaughter, Ayesha Quanette Sanders, Jr. May you be blessed with genius, strength, and a love for learning.

Love always,
Uncle Garry

For my parents who instilled a love of reading within me. For my future children, I hope I can give you the same gift.

Yannie

FUNDO'S ANIMAL ALPHABET

STORY BY GARRY ATKINSON AND AYANA DAVIS

ILLUSTRATED BY GARRY ATKINSON

A is for alligator.

Aa

Amy, the alligator, applauds art.

B is for bear.

Bb

Boogie, the bear, buys blueberries.

C is for camel.

Cc

Connie, the camel, cruises in a caravan.

D is for dog.

Dd

Derek, the dog, digs in his dreams.

E is for elephant. Ee

Eric, the elephant, eats eggplants.

F is for frog.

Ff

Francie, the frog, frolics in the flowers.

G is for giraffe.

Gg

Geoffrey, the giraffe, goes golfing.

H is for hippo.

Hh

Henry, the hippo, hops through hula hoops.

I is for iguana.

Ii

Izzy, the iguana, likes ice cream and insects.

J is for jaguar.

Jj

Jackie, the jaguar, jumps in the jungle.

K is for kangaroo. Kk

Kerry, the kangaroo, knows karate.

L is for lion.

Ll

Leo, the lion, loves licking lollipops.

M is for monkey.

Marco, the monkey, marches on the moon.

N is for numbat. Nn

Nancy, the numbat, notices everything.

O is for octopus. Oo

Oscar, the octopus, occupies the ocean.

P is for pig.

Pp

Percy, the pig, prances in the puddle.

Q is for quail.

Qq

Quincy, the quail, is on a quest for quilts.

R is for rabbit.

Rr

Rosa, the rabbit, rides on a rhinoceros.

S is for snake.

Ss

Steven, the snake, slithers in silence.

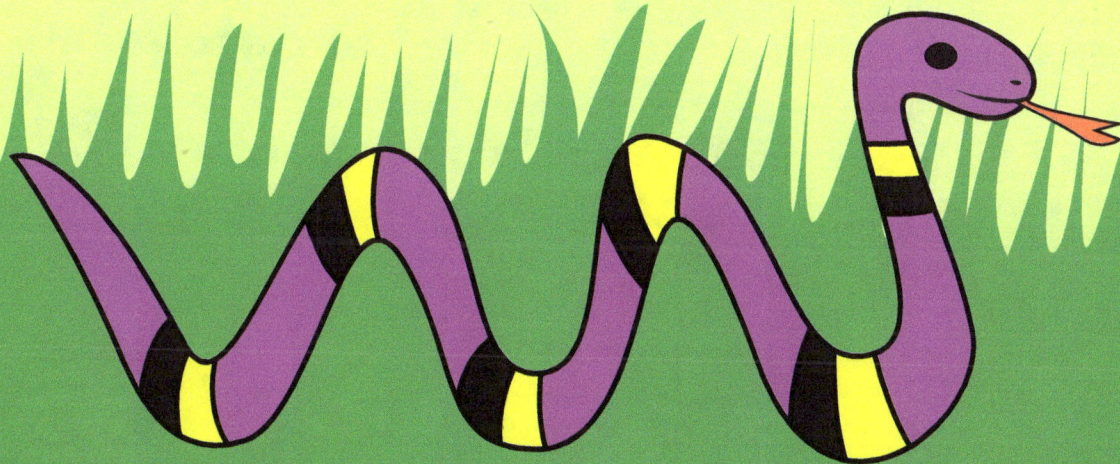

T is for turtle.

Tt

Todd, the turtle, triumphs on the turntables.

U is for urchin. Uu

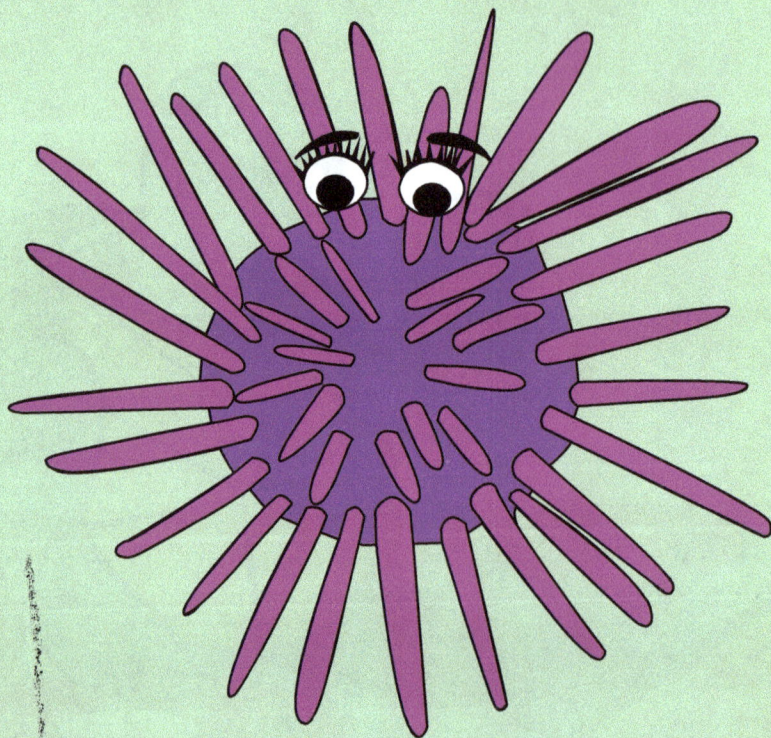

Ursula, the sea urchin, is in a unique uniform.

V is for vulture. Vv

Vincent, the vulture, ventures into the valley.

W is for walrus. Ww

Wilma, the walrus, wears wild wigs.

X is for x-ray fish. Xx

Xavier, the x-ray fish, plays a xylophone.

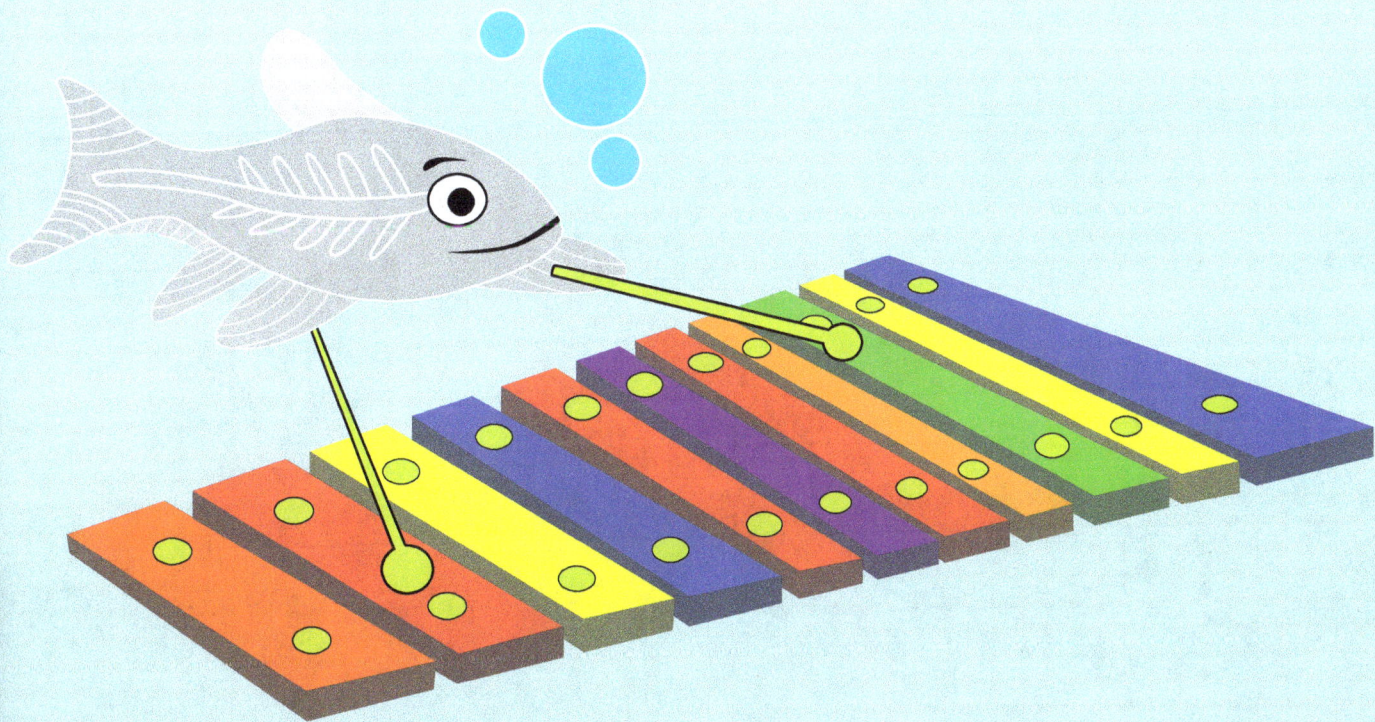

Y is for yak.

Yy

Yvonne, the yak, yearns for yams.

Z is for zebra.

Zz

Zack, the zebra, zips and zigzags through the zoo.

Thanks for joining Fundo on his journey with the animals.

Have fun learning!

Thank you for enjoying "Fundo's Animal Alphabet". Please look for the following books in the Fundo Press family.

"Fundo's 123 Counting"
"Fundo's Shape Story"
"Fundo's Telling Time"
"Fundo's Vegetable Voyage"

For more info, please visit FundoPress.com

We would like to sincerely thank the following people for their contributions in making this book a reality. Your support of "Fundo's Animal Alphabet" is helping to promote learning and creativity to young readers.

LaKela Atkinson
Devin Bridgers
Bobby Bryant
Sheila Burge
Ralph Burgess
Markham Chapel (Durham, NC)
Chris Clearman
Justin Craigwell-Graham
Gwen Davis
Jocelyn Ellis
The Atkinson Family
The Davis Family
Danica Grainger
Takia Hameed
Maxine Hardy
Kieran and Kim Ionescu
Mica Joy
Bettye King
Bhavna Lee
Vivian Lemay
Richard McMillan and Felicia McMillan
Cedric Minor
Dorothy Nelson
Vanessa Brantley Newton
Joan and Paul Pifer
Susan Pitts
Eddie Robinson
Jennifer Wiggins
Janie Woodbridge

Sincerely,
Garry Atkinson and Ayana Davis
Co-Authors

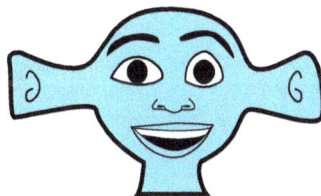

For more info, please visit www.FundoPress.com

FUNDO
PRESS

www.ingramcontent.com/pod-product-compliance
Lightning Source LLC
Chambersburg PA
CBHW081539040426
42447CB00014B/3436